Can You Trust the Bible?

Ralph O. Muncaster

HARVEST HOUSE PUBLISHERS
Eugene, Oregon 97402

3.99

D1048961

Cover by Terry Dugan Design, Minneapolis, Minnesota

By Ralph O. Muncaster

Are There Hidden Codes in the Bible?

Can You Trust the Bible?

Creation vs. Evolution

Creation vs. Evolution Video

How Do We Know Jesus Is God?

Is the Bible Really a Message from God?

What Is the Proof for the Resurrection?

CAN YOU TRUST THE BIBLE?
Copyright © 2000 by Ralph O. Muncaster
Published by Harvest House Publishers
Eugene, Oregon 97402

Library of Congress Cataloging-in-Publication Data

Muncaster, Ralph O.
    Can you trust the Bible? / Ralph O. Muncaster.
        p. cm.—(Examine the evidence series)
    ISBN 0-7369-0355-0
        1. Bible—History. I. Title.

BS445 .M69 2000
220.1—dc21   99-053612

00 01 02 03 04 05 06 07 08 09 / BP/ 10 9 8 7 6 5 4 3 2 1

Contents

Is the Bible Accurate?

Why Does It Matter?

Anyone who knows the content of the Bible knows
that its reliability is the single most important
question in the history of humanity.

Why?

Because the Bible clearly specifies the relationship of human
beings with the God of the universe and what He expects. If the
Bible is accurate, life's most important issues have *direct, clear*
answers:

1. *Quality of life*—Some will find inner peace, others won't.

2. *Life after death*—Some will exist in heaven, the others in hell.

3. *How*—A plan to achieve both of the above is outlined.

Many people have a philosophical belief that goes like this:
"If there really is a God, and if He's good, I just can't believe
He'd 'send' good people to hell." But perhaps this is *human
wishful thinking*. If God's standards of good are different from
human standards (certainly a *perfect God* might have higher
standards), wouldn't it make more sense to attempt to find out
what God's standards are and what He expects? If supernatural
communication from God exists in the Bible revealing *His*
standards, *His* rules, and *His* plan of redemption, wouldn't it be
arrogant and foolish to think human philosophy is more reliable
than the God of the universe? A more intelligent response would
be to verify that the communication is from God, then to *learn
and follow it*.

Fortunately, God has provided abundant proof that the Bible contains His words and ideas inspired in the minds of His selected writers.[1,2,3] This booklet provides evidence not only that the original Bible was inspired by God but that the original inspired books and words are accurate and available to us today in several reliable translations.

It's sad that many intelligent people look to untrustworthy sources for answers, including psychics, astrology, and occult practices. The supernatural evidence of the God of the Bible is vastly more amazing. More importantly, it's consistent, it's certain, and it provides easy directions for fulfillment on earth and in heaven.

The Key Issues

Information in the Bible is so important that we need to know that its words are reliable inspiration from God. Otherwise we might reject it, select only appealing ideas, or change words to make it fit our *wants* . . . not God's instructions. Many religions, cults, and pseudo-Christian groups do just that—interpret (or even rewrite) the Bible in a more appealing way. But a thorough investigation of the reliability of the Bible reveals its divine inspiration, collection, and transmission from the original sources.

Job
Moses
Joshua
Asaph
Samuel
Solomon
Heman
David
Ethan
Joel
Jonah
Hosea
Nahum
Amos
Micah
Habakkuk
Isaiah
Jeremiah
Zephaniah
Obadiah
Daniel
Ezekiel
Zechariah
Haggai
Malachi
Nehemiah
Ezra
Matthew
Mark
Luke
John
Paul
Peter
James
Jude

The Authors and Books

How do we know the authors of the Bible were all inspired by God? Apart from hundreds of prophetic verifications observed by the Israelites, Jesus Christ Himself verified the Scriptures—both the Old Testament (directly) and the New Testament (indirectly) (John 14:26; 16:13). While His authority alone is sufficient, there is other evidence, including scientific insights, fulfilled prophecy, and other manuscript miracles (see pp. 42–45). Even concealed evidence verifies divine revelation throughout the Bible (see pp. 44–45).

The Reliability

How do we know detailed verification by Jesus provides reliable authority? The proof of Jesus' divine authority is confirmed by both 100-percent fulfilled prophecy and, ultimately, by His resurrection (other books in the *Examine the Evidence* series show supporting evidence for this). Additional evidence supports holy Scripture, including eyewitnesses' willingness to die to verify its inspiration and accuracy (see pp. 22–23, 38–41).

The Transmission

The Bible had to be transmitted over centuries from fragile papyrus to more durable paper and more permanent storage conditions. Analysis of ancient documents shows amazing accuracy; manuscripts are virtually unchanged since earliest copies (circa 300 B.C.—see pp. 26–31). Undoubtedly the precise practices of the Jewish scribes (see pp. 18–19) and God's assurance of survival (see pp. 38–41) are responsible for such accurate transmission over the centuries.

How the Bible Fits with History

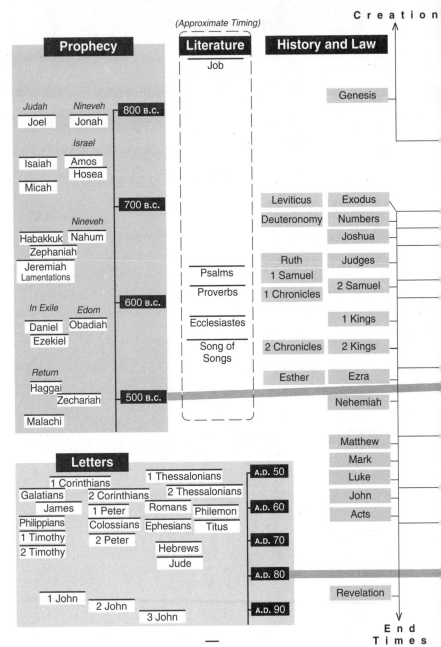

Copper, Bronze
Music, Wheel

F l o o d

Plow Invented
Earliest Civilization
Tigris-Euphrates
Great Pyramids
Egyptians Treat Illness
Abraham   Hieroglyphics
Cuneiform

2000 B.C.   **2000 B.C.**

Isaac
Jacob
Joseph

Shang Dynasty

Hyksos—Egypt

Amenhotep II

1500 B.C. Moses   Pharaoh—Egypt **1500 B.C.**

Parchment
Joshua   Iron
Mycenaeans
Deborah   Minoans
Gideon   Troy Built
Samson   Chinese Chart Stars

1000 B.C. Saul   **1000 B.C.**
David   Disease Thought to Be Caused by Evil Spirits
Solomon
Ahab, Elijah   First Olympics
Elisha   Assyrian Empire
Northern Kingdom Falls   Buddha Born
    60-Unit Math System
Fall of Jerusalem   Babylonian Empire
EXILE   Persian Empire

500 B.C.   **500 B.C.**
Disease Attributed to Natural Cause

Between Testaments   Aristotle: Earth—Center
(No Biblical Record)   Geometry, Mathematics
Lever and Pulley

0   **0**

Tiberius Caesar
J E S U S   Public Health Improved:
Aqueducts, Sewage

Paul Encounters Christ
Peter Imprisoned
A.D. 50 Paul's First Mission   **A.D. 50**
Paul's Second Mission
Paul's Third Mission   Nero—Fire of Rome
Jerusalem Destroyed

A.D. 80   Pompeii Destroyed   **A.D. 80**
John Exiled   Ptolemy—"Earth Center" Theory, Counts Stars

A.D. 100   Paper Invented   **A.D. 100**

First Medicine—Based on Experiment

Old Testament History
Early Records

The earliest portions of the Bible may have been recorded as early as Abraham (about 2000 B.C.). The events of Job are believed to have occurred about Abraham's time in Mesopotamia—an area where writing was well developed. Abraham's hometown of Ur was a center of education. Clay tablets have been discovered in Ur that record various contracts, teaching methods, and advanced mathematics. Abraham, from a family of wealth, was probably highly educated. It's conceivable that manuscripts of Job (or other records) were passed from Abraham to Moses through heirs—though no supporting evidence has been found yet. Animal skins were used to record state documents as early as 3000 B.C., making it possible that Abraham (a nomad) possessed such portable written documents.

Moses and the Historical Books

Moses wrote the first five books of the Bible (the Torah), spanning creation, the patriarchs, the exodus from Egypt (about 1450 B.C.), and the revealing of the Law. Writing at the time of Moses was quite advanced, especially in Egypt. Hieroglyphics were often written on parchment, a specially prepared animal skin that was more durable than papyrus (a paper-like substance made from reeds from the Nile). Moses, educated in the best Egyptian schools, would certainly have had the ability to write.

In the late 1800s, critical scholars believed that Moses could not have written the first five books of the Bible since, they argued, writing had not developed adequately for such a "Law." In 1901, the Code of Hammurabi was discovered. Written as law in Babylon prior to 1750 B.C., it verified that even other cultures had advanced systems of writing and law. Also in the 1800s, "higher criticism" claimed that use of different "names" of God in the Torah indicated different authors. Substantial research[4, 5, 6] has soundly refuted that idea as well. The Bible and even Jesus clearly indicate Moses' authorship (see Exodus 24:4; Deuteronomy 31:9; Mark 10:5; 12:19; Luke 20:28; John 1:45; 5:46).

Other historical books—Joshua, Judges, Ruth, Samuel, Chronicles, Kings, Esther, Nehemiah and Ezra—were written by scribes, whose duty was to maintain the holy record. Historical books of the Bible preserved God's relationship with the Israelites and often contained prophecy.

Books of Wisdom Literature

Although Job is considered a literature book (written about 2000 B.C.), and some Psalms were written as early as the time of Moses or as late as 400 B.C., most literature books were written about 1000 B.C. Key literature authors were King Solomon, who wrote Proverbs, Ecclesiastes, and Song of Songs; and David, who wrote most of the Psalms. Literary books were regarded as Scripture quite early.

The Bible: Good and Bad Revealed!

A degree of authenticity is given to the biblical record by the many unflattering facts given in detail about prominent people and leaders. Then, as today, leaders would prefer that the historical record reflect the good, but not the bad. Records of other nations avoided such issues as murder, adultery, and scandals by leaders.

Old Testament History
Prophecy and Structure

Books of Prophecy

Like books of history, most books of prophecy are believed to have been written by scribes of the prophets (or even the prophets themselves). Prophecy was extremely important to the people of Israel and was regarded as a vital test of "someone speaking of God." Hence, whenever a prophet spoke in the name of God (as in "thus saith the Lord") it was deemed "of God", and consequences were very serious if prophecy did not come true. Unlike today's psychics and fortune tellers, prophets in biblical times were required by the Law to be stoned to death if their prophecy did not come true.

Consequently, the content of the books of prophecy had to be 100-percent accurate to qualify as prophecy. Perfect fulfillment emphasized both short-term and long-term prophecies to verify God's inspiration. Short-term prophecy quickly identified false prophets (who would make mistakes). Long-term prophecies have   helped later generations believe in divine revelation.

Old Testament Organization

Today the books of the Old Testament are organized (basically) chronologically within three divisions: History and Law, Literature, and Prophecy. Early Hebrews (and Jews today) have three similar groupings: the Law (first five books), the Prophets, and the Writings. The Hebrews included some historical "books" among the Prophets (Joshua, Judges, Samuel, Kings) and others within the "Writings" (Ruth, Esther, Ezra-Nehemiah, and Chronicles). The Torah (Law) had a defined order—as it does today. Scholars believe all other scrolls were grouped in containers with no particular order. When the "codex" (book form) was developed in the first century, a definite order was necessary. The Hebrew Bible appears to be in the order in which the books became "canonized," which accounts for such inconsistencies as Chronicles being at the end, even though the events took place before Ezra-Nehemiah. Jesus knew and referred to the *traditional* order, as indicated by His reference to the first and last martyrs (Abel and Zechariah—see Matthew 23:35). Second Chronicles shows Zechariah as the "last" martyr. However, historically, Uriah was the last martyr (Jeremiah 26:23).

New Testament History

The New Testament is generally grouped as follows:

1. the Gospel accounts
(Matthew, Mark, Luke and John)
along with Acts,

2. the letters, and

3. Revelation.

The Gospels and Acts were written for the purpose of evangelism (telling others the "good news" story of Jesus). The letters were written for the purpose of special instruction (for the church body—and various other reasons). Revelation is a special book that clarifies events leading to the ultimate victory of Christ over Satan. Using vivid, highly symbolic language, it paints a picture of a glorious new kingdom, and offers assurance of eternal rewards for all Christians.

The Gospel Accounts

The Gospel accounts were written by Matthew (a disciple—the tax collector), Mark (a "scribe" of Peter), Luke (Paul's doctor, who also wrote Acts—considered an "extension" of Luke), and John (a favorite disciple of Jesus). Some believe the Gospels were all written entirely independently, with the Holy Spirit prompting writers to record identical information. Others believe they were developed using *some* of the same sources. Critics of the Bible sometimes suggest that different sources might imply unreliability. More likely, *it implies reliability*. Even today, *multiple* independent sources are considered the best evidence of truth.

Luke tells us that many people had been *writing* about the events of the life of Jesus (Luke 1:1). He also indicates he is making a careful investigation of the facts using other reliable writings and eyewitness testimony (Luke 1:2-4). Hence, Luke carefully and thoroughly researched *both* written and spoken testimony from eyewitnesses to provide an orderly account of the ministry of Jesus.

Scholars believe Luke's sources included the Gospel of Mark (believed to be the first Gospel written).[7, 8, 9, 10] Most information contained in Mark is included in both Matthew (606 common verses) and Luke (350 verses). A second source, which scholars call "Q," is believed to have been used by both Matthew and Luke (200 common verses).[9, 10] Due to similarities, these three books are referred to as the "synoptic gospels" (from the Greek word *synopsis,* which means "a seeing together"). Although writers of the Gospels investigated various eyewitness sources, there is evidence (consistency and divine insights) that the Holy Spirit prompted the final words of each writing—just as Jesus indicated (John 14:26).

Both the differences and the similarities of the Gospels are important indications of trustworthiness. If only similarities existed, a common source might be considered biased or faulty. If only differences existed, reconciliation could be difficult. The consistent reporting of similarities and differences of *eyewitness testimony* lends credibility to the message—as it would in a court of law today.

All Gospels were completed, widely circulated, and accepted as Scripture well within the lifetime of eyewitnesses. Most scholars believe the writing of the actual Gospels occurred 10 to 35 years after the resurrection (or A.D. 40 to A.D. 65). This does not mean, however, that other records did not exist in various written forms before then. Luke confirms that many writings existed (Luke 1:1).

The Letters

Letters were written to various churches and individuals by Paul and others to: 1) clarify the ministry of Christ, 2) guide the early church, and 3) encourage others to become Christlike. Long before the end of the first century, Paul's letters were circulated as a group and were considered Scripture by the early church. Like the prophets of the Old Testament, Paul claimed to be speaking for God (1 Thessalonians 2:13; 5:27; 1 Corinthians 14:37; Colossians 4:16). Clement of Rome indicates his support of various New Testament books as Scripture by liberally referring to the Gospels of Matthew and Luke, and to several letters (Hebrews, Romans, Corinthians, 1 Timothy, Titus, 1 Peter, Ephesians) in a letter to Christians in Corinth in A.D. 95.[7,8]

Revelation

Written on the island of Patmos in about A.D. 95 by John, Revelation is full of highly symbolic language. Scholars believe a reason for this style was to help protect the book during a period of intense persecution—making it a less obvious Christian target. The book of Revelation describes "end times" events and promises a new kingdom with eternal rewards for all Christians. John claims Revelation is from God (Revelation 1:1-3).

The Canon

Canon simply means "standardized." But in biblical understanding, it has the special importance of implying Scripture is from God, or "God-breathed." There is substantial evidence from historical writings that indicates the canon of the Old Testament was essentially "closed" (determined) no later than 167 B.C.[7,8] Jesus referred frequently to the Scriptures as if they were a preordained collection of words from God. No room for variance was ever suggested. The Old Testament canon was officially approved by the Jews in A.D. 70.

The Final (Closed) Canon

The church had essentially determined a canon (an accepted collection of books) for the entire Bible by A.D. 200 (see p. 17). This became official in A.D. 397. Although church history is filled with debate over issues, every time a canon became official, it simply confirmed a canon already in existence. It seems God controlled the process. Today, most Christians consider it closed or unchangeable (Deuteronomy 4:2; Revelation 22:18).

Isaiah Foretold Gospel Development

Several times Isaiah indicated God would intervene in history through a Messiah (Isaiah 40:9; 52:7; 61:1). The Hebrew word *bâsar* was used to indicate this coming "day of the Lord." Greek translators (280 B.C.) believed the best translation was the same word that means "gospel," or "good news." Hence the coming of the Messiah was forever linked to the gospel as prophesied by Jesus in the New Testament (see Mark 1:14,15; 1 Corinthians 15).

The Official Canon

The First Canon

The first five books of the Bible (Torah) were believed to be officially recognized as "from God" shortly after the return of the Jews from exile (about 500 B.C.).[7] Moses' status as a prophet, however, would indicate his writings were considered holy long before they were officially recognized.

Old Testament Canon

Evidence shows the Hebrews accepted the current Old Testament books as Scripture by 167 B.C.[7,8] In Jesus' day, there was no doubt about the books of Scripture. Final recognition of the Hebrew canon was not made until A.D. 70.

The Final Canon

While most New Testament books were accepted as Scripture at least by the early 200s, final confirmation of today's canon was not until the Council of Carthage in A.D. 397. Much earlier, Origen, writing in the early 200s, listed all 27 books of the current New Testament (but indicated six* were of questionable status).

* The six in question were Hebrews, James, 2 Peter, 2 and 3 John, and Jude.

Reliability of Transmission

Understanding the reliable transmission of the Bible requires breaking out of the twentieth-century mindset. Today we often regard other documents far above religious writings.

Role of Holy Scripture

Holy Scripture was of *extreme* importance to the early Hebrews. The theocracy of Israel (ruled by God) looked to Scripture for its laws, its spiritual guidance, and its hope for the future. Even though the nation was often disobedient, holy Scripture was always held in high esteem.

Examples of the Reverence of Scripture

- **The name of God**—Fearing "use of God's name in vain," scribes altered its spelling. Every time God's name was written, a "sanctification verse" was spoken by the scribe.

- **Insistence on precision**—The all-important "master scrolls" (from which copies were made) were cross-checked in many ways (see p. 19, "Scriptural Copy Rules").

- **Ceremonial burial**—The sacred books were so highly valued that when they eventually wore out, they were given a ceremonial burial. Some of these buried copies have been found.

The importance of holy Scripture in the culture made it virtually impossible to deliberately insert inaccuracies. All scrolls would have had to be changed simultaneously—along with countless memories—just to make one single change.

Scriptural Copy Rules

Stringent rules concerning materials used, technique, and format were followed. Scribes (the word literally means "counters") verified precision by these methods:

- Total letters in a scroll were counted (verified).

- Each individual letter was counted (verified).

- Words were counted and totalled per scroll.

- The middle letter of each scroll was found (by counting) and verified against the master.[6]

If there was a single mistake, the entire "replacement" master scroll was destroyed.

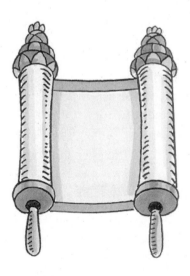

Jesus Confirmed the Bible

Was every *book*, every *author*, every *word* of the Bible inspired by God? It's certainly impossible to prove. But just consider:

A God . . .

- who supernaturally created the entire universe,*

- who foretold the future with perfect accuracy,*

- who gave scientific insights thousands of years in advance,*

- who placed evidence in the Bible concealed for centuries,*

Could certainly . . .

- put word-for-word ideas into the mind of human authors.

- inspire His "chosen people" to select the right books for His Word.

Jesus Confirmed the Old Testament

The Old Testament Hebrew Scriptures were fully developed and effectively canonized by 167 B.C. (pp. 16–17). If there were incorrect books, false prophecies, or errors, Jesus would certainly *not* have regarded them as holy Scripture. Jesus was quick to point out the errors of the "establishment," but was very consistent in His support of holy Scripture. For example, in the New Testament:

- Jesus refers to Scripture as an authority 56 times.

- Jesus quotes directly from Scripture, implying even that specific words are from God, more than 81 times.

- Twenty books are quoted—more than half of today's Old Testament. Using the Hebrew organization of Jesus' day, all but four books are quoted (p. 34).

* Subjects explored in greater detail in other books of the *Examine the Evidence* series.

- Jesus verifies details. Jesus specifies that not the slightest detail will disappear from the Law until everything is accomplished (Matthew 5:18). He further specifies that everything in the Law of Moses, the prophets, and the Psalms (the three categories of the Hebrew Bible) will be fulfilled (Luke 24:44).

Jesus Confirmed the Gospel

While on earth, Jesus gave authority to the apostles to write the *New Testament*, then further prophesied and confirmed it.

- Authority was granted—the Holy Spirit was to guide the very words of the apostles (John 14:26; 16:13; Luke 12:12; Acts 1:8).

- The gospel was prophesied—17 times Jesus prophesied that the apostles would provide the gospel (see Matthew 24:14; 26:13; Mark 8:35; Luke 21:33; Acts 16-18).

- The gospel was confirmed while it was preached—three times Jesus confirmed testimony as it was occurring (Acts 18:9; 22:18; 23:11).

Why Is Jesus an Authority?

There is substantial evidence that Jesus is the divine Son of God. All-knowing, like God the Father, Jesus is the ultimate authority of truth. Skeptics may refer to other books in the *Examine the Evidence* series.

Other Evidence of Bible Books and Authors

The Old Testament

Of course, nothing more is needed than the confirmation of the Old Testament by Jesus. However, for the skeptic there is other evidence of God's inspiration.

- *The apostles confirmed it.* There are 212 references to Old Testament Scripture in 17 books of the New Testament. Paul specifically states that all Scripture is "God-breathed" (2 Timothy 3:16).

- *Devout eyewitnesses confirmed it.* The Israelites were an intensely devout nation. A single error of prophecy caused the "prophet" to be stoned to death (and his work would not be regarded as Scripture). Most of the books of the Old Testament contain prophecy that was regarded as certain proof that something was of God (Deuteronomy 18:20-22, Isaiah 41:22,23).

- *Miraculous insight confirms it.* There is substantial evidence of God's authorship throughout the Old Testament, including miraculously fulfilled prophecy, scientific insights thousands of years before their discovery, concealed evidence throughout the Bible, and the precise, accurate account of creation.*

The New Testament

Again, the preauthorization and prophecies by Jesus for the New Testament are the most important evidence of its reliability. Yet other facts verify it as well:

* Detailed in other books in the *Examine the Evidence* series.

- *Eyewitnesses confirmed it.* Imagine if today news reports said a person claiming to be God rose from the dead. Such a story would demand considerable confirmation before it would be taken seriously. Certainly a rumor would not survive strict scrutiny by eyewitnesses if it were false. If true, it might become an amazing classic. This describes the New Testament. The account was widely circulated while eyewitnesses were alive. Its circulation vastly exceeded that of any other document ever written (pp. 26–27).

- *Death verified it.* Martyrdom for a *cause* is not new. Martyrdom for a known *lie* would be insane. All apostles certainly *knew* the truth and died violent deaths (except John) to verify the account.

- *The early church believed it.* The Gospels and letters were considered Scripture—equal to the Old Testament.[7, 8]

Jesus' Warning: Trust Scripture

Some skeptical people may not fully appreciate the importance of trusting Scripture. Some may "pick and choose" only appealing parts of the Bible—or, worse, not truly accept the claims of Jesus Christ as Lord and Savior.

Jesus gives us a vivid warning against rejecting the words of Moses and the prophets when He indicates that people not listening to them would not be convinced of the horror of hell even if someone "rises from the dead" (Luke 16:27-31).

Jesus also emphasized the accuracy of Scripture down to the smallest detail (Matthew 5:18).

Milestones of Bible Development

Dead Sea Scrolls Written

The earliest scrolls were copied by 300 B.C., and many before 200 B.C. This verifies that the prophecies of Christ were recorded long before His birth (p. 28).

Moses Writes Law

History Books Written

Most Literature Books Written

Prophecy Books Written

Septuagint Written

Almost 300 years before Christ's birth, the Old Testament was translated into Greek. Early copies still exist today, providing further assurance the Old Testament has remained virtually unchanged since the time of Jesus (p. 29).

Letters Written

Gospels Written

Hebrew Canon (Unofficial)

By 167 B.C. the Old Testament text, matching the Hebrew text of today, was considered "God-breathed" Scripture. Evidence confirms today's Old Testament books match those used by Christ. Hebrew canon became official in A.D. 70 (p. 17).

Letters Become Scripture

Within the lifetime of the apostles many of the letters were already given status equal to the Old Testament. Shortly after, the Gospels were also deemed Scripture (p. 13–23).

Miraculous Design	Miraculous Survival	Miraculous Insights
With more than 40 authors of vastly different backgrounds, over 1500 years, on different continents, the Bible is miraculously integrated and consistent (pp. 36–37).	*Never* has a book been so intensely persecuted. *Never* have odds of survival been so slim. And *never* has the evidence been so great (pp. 26,27,38–41).	Profound insights are within the Bible—*not* found in any other holy book (pp. 42–45): prophecy miracles, scientific insights, and concealed evidence.

Dead Sea Scrolls Buried

A devout sect of Jews, the Essenes, buried hundreds of scrolls in caves in Qumran just prior to the fall of Jerusalem in A.D. 70. All Old Testament books, except Esther, were preserved. Recently released scrolls have evidence of the New Testament and the crucifixion.

Christ Confirms Scripture

Certainly Christ would have voiced any problems regarding authors, books, or content of Scripture. To the contrary, Jesus confirmed authority of Scripture down to the smallest detail (p. 20).

Dead Sea Scrolls Discovered

In 1947, the first Dead Sea Scrolls were discovered, untouched for nearly 2000 years. As with a time capsule, comparison with current Hebrew texts reveals today's Bible is consistent with the Scripture in Jesus' day. Analysis shows amazing accuracy after centuries (p. 28).

- Rylands (p. 30)
- Bodmer (p. 30)
- Chester Beatty (p. 30)
- Codex Vaticanus (p. 30)
- Codex Sinaiticus (p. 30)
- Vulgate (p. 30)

Gospels as Scripture

Precisely as prophesied by Christ, the New Testament Gospel accounts were widely circulated and quickly deemed of equal status to Scripture (pp. 13–14).

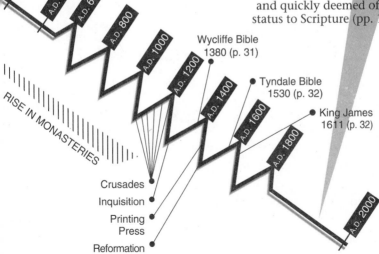

A.D. 400
A.D. 500
A.D. 600
A.D. 800
A.D. 1000
A.D. 1200
A.D. 1400
A.D. 1600
A.D. 1800
A.D. 2000

RISE IN MONASTERIES

Wycliffe Bible 1380 (p. 31)

Tyndale Bible 1530 (p. 32)

King James 1611 (p. 32)

Crusades
Inquisition
Printing Press
Reformation

The Manuscript "Explosion"

No work has survived and spread as the gospel has.
*Something **major** happened.*

Background—Manuscript Deterioration

To fully appreciate the miraculous survival of ancient biblical documents, we must realize how easily words written on ancient materials deteriorated and were lost forever. Consider your family's most cherished documents—birth certificates, marriage licenses, key contracts. How many still exist? While modern paper and storage far surpass the technology of ancient times, we still lose most documents. In ancient times materials were much more fragile and storage conditions much worse. Problems included:

Typical Problems	Additional Bible Problems
• Fragile materials (papyrus, parchment)	• Intentional destruction
• Poor storage (weather)	• Fear of copying
• Time (loss of documents)	• Martyrdom

Consequently, we have very few ancient manuscripts of *anything*. Many historical works—widely referenced by others—have vanished completely.

The Explosion of the Gospel

There were *no* printing presses, *no* photocopiers, *no* quick ways to copy manuscripts. Nevertheless, the Gospel quickly expanded throughout the Roman Empire. Comprehending the scale of this vast explosion of hand-copied documents is only possible by comparing the number of extant New Testament manuscripts with those of other abundant documents.

Number of Surviving Ancient Manuscripts[6]

• *New Testament*	▦▦▦▦▦▦▦▦▦▦▦▦▦▦▦▦▦▦▦▦▦▦ ▦▦▦▦▦▦▦ **24,000+** ▦▦▦▦▦▦▦▦▦▦▦▦▦ ▦▦▦▦▦▦▦ **copies** ▦▦▦▦▦▦▦▦▦▦▦ ▦▦▦▦▦▦▦▦▦▦▦▦▦▦▦▦▦▦▦▦▦▦
• *Iliad* (second-most abundant)—Homer	▦▦▦▦▦ **643** **copies**
• *Gallic Wars* —Julius Caesar	▦ **10** **copies**
• *Historical Works* —Herodotus	▦ **8** **copies**
• *Historical Works* —Thucydides	▦ **8** **copies**
• *Historical Works* —Pliny the Younger	▦ **7** **copies**

> Why do some doubt biblical accuracy, yet readily accept other, less reliable history?

What Does This Mean?

Having more surviving early manuscripts means having more cross-checks to verify accuracy. Today's Bible is verified to a textual accuracy of 99.5 percent, compared with 95 percent for the *best* other ancient work (The *Iliad*).[4]

Some biblical copies are old enough to show eyewitnesses' confirmation *(made within 25 years of events)*.

Earliest copies (after autographs) of others:

Iliad .... 500 years	*Gallic Wars* .... 1000 years
Herodotus .... 1300 years	*Thucydides* .... 1300 years
	Pliny the Younger .. 750 years

Ancient Manuscripts
Verify Accuracy

Until this century, the earliest Old Testament copies were from about A.D. 1000 (similar to typical historical works—see previous page). Skeptics argued textual corruption was possible. Others argued miracles of prophecy—especially concerning Jesus—were recorded centuries after Christ and were changed to fit the outcome of history. Modern archaeological discoveries soundly refute such claims. Thousands of much earlier documents now verify biblical accuracy.

Dead Sea Scrolls

Perhaps the most important archaeological find in history is the discovery of the Dead Sea Scrolls in 1947–48. Discovered accidently by a Bedouin shepherd searching a cave in the Qumran region near the Dead Sea, the scrolls had been hidden by the Essenes (a Jewish sect similar to the Pharisees and Sadducees) just prior to the fall of Jerusalem in A.D. 70. It took almost 20 years to uncover all scrolls and bring them together in one location.

The discovery includes thousands of fragments and some complete scrolls found in 11 caves. In total, about 800 scrolls have been identified, which include copies of every book of the Old Testament (except Esther), along with a number of other scrolls relevant to history and to the Essene community. Several scrolls exist in multiple copies. Many of the oldest scrolls (including the remarkably intact scroll of Isaiah) were written more than 200 years before Christ—long before the fulfillment of prophecies they contain about the coming Messiah.[4, 5, 6, 7, 8, 9, 11, 12]

New Testament Evidence

For years, many of the Dead Sea scrolls were not released by the government of Israel. Recently released fragments and scrolls clearly refer to an awareness of a suffering Messiah who was crucified as a Savior. Some scholars show evidence of fragments from the books of Mark, Acts, Romans, 1 Timothy and James. Another recently released scroll called the "Son of God Scroll" contains some of the exact wording from the Gospel of Luke (Luke 1:32-35). This implies that much of the New Testament was written before A.D. 70.[11]

Ancient Translations

Septuagint—This was the original translation of the Old Testament and other apocryphal books into Greek, which was made from about 285 B.C. to 270 B.C. Several early copies still survive today, providing additional early verification.

Other Translations—A translation of the Gospels into Christian Aramaic (Syriac) was produced from A.D. 150 to A.D. 250. Some 15 other language translations shortly followed. Hundreds of early versions have survived from the early 400s.

The Crucified Messiah Scroll

A Dead Sea scroll released in 1991 spoke of a Messiah who "suffered crucifixion for the sins of men." Also included were references to Isaiah 53, tying this Messiah to the suffering servant Isaiah foretold centuries before.[11] Ironically, some Jewish sects have actually removed Isaiah 53 from Scripture—its reference is "too" descriptive of Jesus. This find, however, indicates the people of Jesus' day were well aware of, and accepted, the parallel.

Other Manuscripts . . .

In addition to the Dead Sea Scrolls and Septuagint, some of the most important biblical writings, of the thousands available, are the following:

Rylands Papyrus (A.D. 115–A.D.125)—A very early fragment showing early authorship of the book of John.

Bodmer Papyri (A.D. 150–A.D. 200)—Additional portions of the Gospels of John and Luke.

Chester Beatty Papyri (A.D. 100–A.D. 300)—Portions of all major sections of the New Testament are intact (all Gospels, Acts, Epistles, Revelation).

Codex Vaticanus (Early 300s)—Earliest *nearly complete* Bible written in Greek on vellum (a form of animal hide more durable than papyrus). Portions of the Old Testament pastoral letters and parts of Hebrews and Revelation are lost. Housed in the Vatican since at least 1481, it was not available to scholars until the 1900s. It is considered one of the most accurate biblical manuscripts currently available.

Codex Sinaiticus (Early 300s)—The earliest known complete New Testament. Written in Greek, it was discovered in 1859 in St. Catherine's Monastery at the base of Mount Sinai.

The Vulgate (A.D. 400)—The key "standardized translation" of the Bible into Latin by Jerome, the leading biblical scholar of his day. In addition to "Old Latin" versions, Jerome used Greek and Hebrew manuscripts for final translation. It included books of apocrypha (pp. 34–35), and for centuries it was the only Bible recognized by the Roman Catholic Church.

The Church and the English Bible

The Roman Catholic Church dominated the expansion of Christianity for many years. This influence had tremendous positive impact (much of the evangelism, teaching and recordkeeping we highly value today is a result of Roman Catholic efforts). During this time, monasteries were the centers for education and for the tedious work of copying biblical manuscripts. However, the church also had dark times (1300s–1600s) when it fell into a time of general apostasy, corruption, and political control . . . a time when "indulgences" were sold (supposedly to provide salvation), positions were "bought," and the innocent were persecuted.

During this time the Catholic Church opposed translation of the Bible into English. By insisting on Latin (the Vulgate), the Catholic Church had ultimate control over the common people's understanding of Scripture (most did not know Latin).

Wycliffe's Bible (A.D. 1383)—John Wycliffe, a Catholic, believed Christ was the true head of the Catholic Church, not the pope. He (with associates) produced the first English translation of the Vulgate and distributed it in England. Condemned by Pope Gregory XI, he might well have been executed if not for his political influence during the time of the Hundred Years' War with France (later his bones were dug up, burned, and thrown into the river Swift).

Historical Development

The Reformation (1500s)

The Church, generally recognizing its problems, entered a period of correction. Unfortunately, too much emphasis is often given to the birth of Protestant churches during this time and not enough emphasis to overall church reformation. This misunderstanding has resulted in needless conflict. Within the period, important Bible translations were made, and the roles of some "apocrypha" were defined.

Tyndale Bible (1530)—William Tyndale was the first to translate the entire Bible from the original languages of Hebrew, Aramaic and Greek into English (others completed it after his martyrdom —next page).

King James (1611)—This translation, relying heavily on the Vulgate, became the new standard Bible for centuries. Fifty-four scholars translated the Vulgate, referencing other Hebrew and Greek texts. It is still considered one of the best translations.

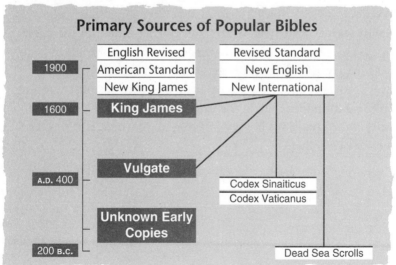

Primary Sources of Popular Bibles

English Revised, American Standard, New King James (1885–1979)— These are modern language translations of the King James Bible. *The English Revised* appeals to the British and the *American Standard* to Americans.

Note: As trustworthy as the original King James Bible is, recent archeological findings including the Dead Sea Scrolls, the Codex Sinaiticus, the Codex Vaticanus, and many other manuscripts give today's scholars added insight. Some *new translations* use the early manuscripts in addition to the King James sources.

Revised Standard (1929, 1990), *New English* (1946, 1970), *New International Version* (1973, 1984)—These Bibles are translations directly from the earliest Hebrew and Greek manuscripts, incorporating insight from intermediate translations. The Catholic counterpart is the New American Bible (1970).

Living Bible (1972), *Good News* (1976), *The Message* (1995)—These "Bibles" paraphrase the literally translated Bibles. They attempt to present ideas in the most relevant language for modern culture. Though they are an easy way to understand the basic teaching, they are not suggested for detailed Bible study since they are human paraphrases of God's literal Word.

Translation Martyr

The Catholic Church opposed translation of the Bible into English. Insisting on Latin (the Vulgate), the Church had ultimate control over interpretation.

William Tyndale was forced to flee to Germany to complete his translation directly from Hebrew and Greek sources. He was condemned by the king, captured, strangled, and burned at the stake for "heresy." His final words were, "Lord, open the King of England's eyes." Two years later (1537), Henry VIII broke off ties with the pope and gave a version of Tyndale's Bible "royal approval."

Structure of Today's Bible

Almost all of the Christian world today accepts the basic canon of the Bible. It consists of 66 books, including an Old Testament identical in content to the Hebrew Bible (though differing in grouping), and New Testament according to the final canon (p. 17). The only significant difference of opinion is regarding the Apocrypha (see below) which is accepted in varying degrees by Protestants, Roman Catholics, and Greek Orthodox churches.

The Apocrypha

Apocrypha literally means "hidden works." Many apocryphal books exist, far in excess of those now incorporated into the Catholic Bible (see insert). Apocryphal

Old Testament Versions

Hebrew	Protestant	Roman Catholic
The Law	*The Law*	*Pentateuch*
Genesis	Genesis	Genesis
Exodus	Exodus	Exodus
Leviticus	Leviticus	Leviticus
Numbers	Numbers	Numbers
Deuteronomy	Deuteronomy	Deuteronomy
The Prophets	*Historical Books*	*Historical Books*
Joshua	Joshua	Joshua
Judges	Judges	Judges
Samuel	Ruth	Ruth
Kings	1 Samuel	1 Samuel
Isaiah	2 Samuel	2 Samuel
Jeremiah	1 Kings	1 Kings
Ezekiel	2 Kings	2 Kings
The Twelve	1 Chronicles	1 Chronicles
The Writings	2 Chronicles	2 Chronicles
Psalms	Ezra	Ezra
Proverbs	Nehemiah	Nehemiah
Job	Esther	Tobit*
Song of Songs		Judith*
Ruth	*Literature*	Esther
Lamentations	Job	1 Maccabees*
Ecclesiastes	Psalms	2 Maccabees*
Esther	Proverbs	
Daniel	Ecclesiastes	*Literature*
Ezra-Nehemiah	Song of Songs	Job
Chronicles		Psalms
	Prophets	Proverbs
	Isaiah	Ecclesiastes
Note: Books of the	Jeremiah	Song of Songs
Hebrew Bible	Lamentations	Wisdom*
contain identical	Ezekiel	Sirach*
information to the	Daniel	(Ecclesiasticus)
Protestant Old	Hosea	
Testament.	Joel	*Prophets*
Organization of	Amos	Isaiah
content is	Obadiah	Jeremiah
different. And	Jonah	Lamentations
some Hebrew	Micah	Baruch*
books contain	Nahum	Ezekiel
several Protestant	Habakkuk	Daniel
books.	Zephaniah	Hosea
	Haggai	Joel
	Zechariah	Amos
	Malachi	Obadiah
		Jonah
		Micah
		Nahum
		Habakkuk
		Zephaniah
		Haggai
		Zechariah
* apocryphal		Malachi

books were *not* considered holy Scripture in Jesus' day, but were still recognized as edifying, and some were regarded as worthy of reading in the church.[7, 8] Even the Septuagint authors translated books of apocrypha. Yet there is substantial evidence that virtually no leaders of the early church considered these books "God-breathed."

Originally, apocryphal books were part of early Protestant Bibles (even in Luther's translation). As in Jesus' time, they were considered profitable but not inspired by God. Eventually, lack of interest and cost caused apocryphal books to disappear from Protestant Bibles, but they remained in Catholic versions.

It was not until 1546 that the Roman Catholic Church gave the apocryphal books in its Bible "deuterocanonical," or secondary status. Protestants disagree with that status.

Selecting the Canon

Biblical canon is intended to include only works that were inspired by God. Primary considerations were: Was it . . .

- *Authoritative*—Divinely inspired?

- *Prophetic*—100-percent fulfilled prophecy?

- *Authentic*—Documents known to be valid?

- *Dynamic*—Life-transforming guidance?

- *Acceptable*—Consistent with God's nature?

Miraculous Authorship

How rare is it today to see two different authors write articles on controversial topics—like sexual conduct, men and women's roles, or life after death—that agree *point by point?* Even today, in one city in one culture, it rarely happens.

Now consider the Bible. This writing took place from about 2000 B.C. to A.D. 100. It consists of 66 books written by at least 40

Diverse—Yet Consistent—Books of the Bible

Approx. Date	Probable Author	Book(s)	Author's Occupation	Where Written	Circumstances
2000 B.C.	Job	Job	Wealthy farmer	Mesopotamia	General peace
1450	Moses	TORAH++	Political leader	Wilderness	Wandering
1400	Joshua	Joshua	Military general	Canaan	War
1000	Samuel	Samuel	Prophet	Canaan	Internal strife
1000	David	Psalms	Shepherd, king	Fields, palace	Conflict
970	Solomon	Proverbs+	King	Palace	Peace
750	Amos	Amos	Herdsman	Fields	Pre-exile
600	Jeremiah	Jeremiah+	Prophet	Dungeon	Depression
535	Daniel	Daniel	Prime minister	Hillside, palace	Exile
440	Nehemiah	Nehemiah	Cupbearer	Jerusalem	Rebuilding
A.D. 35–60	Mark	Mark	Scribe	Jerusalem	Early Christian
40–65	Matthew	Matthew	Tax collector	Jerusalem	Early Christian
40–65	Luke	Luke+	Physician	Rome	Early Christian
60–90	John	John+	Fisherman	Asia	Early Christian
45–64	Paul	Letters+	Rabbi	Prison	Persecution
60–64	Peter	Letters+	Fisherman	Rome	Persecution

+ More than one book written
++ First 5 books: Genesis, Exodus, Leviticus, Numbers, Deuteronomy

authors, from vastly different cultures, vastly different backgrounds, in different locations, and in different circumstances.

Yet, the Bible is consistent throughout on thousands of highly controversial issues.

Why?

Perhaps the Bible had just one author. Perhaps it was the God of the universe—just as the creators of the canon believed. Perhaps there is truth to the claim that the Holy Spirit not only directed the prophets, the gospel writers, and the organizers of the Bible, but the very words themselves. Certainly the miraculous survival, the miraculous "fingerprints" of God, would support the notion that God wants to provide a tool to communicate to His people (see pp. 42–45).

Most Surprising Author?

King Nebuchadnezzar, the tyrant of Babylon who conquered Israel and exiled the Jews (586 B.C.), was the author of the fourth chapter of Daniel. His story shows how God can change the hearts of even the most unlikely people. As prophesied, the king became insane and was dethroned for seven years. Turning to God, he regained power, greater than before.

Miraculous Survival . . .

There are many great writings of history that we have lost forever. We know about them because other surviving documents refer to them. Even the Bible speaks of books we cannot locate (see 1 Chronicles 9:1; 2 Chronicles 20:34; Nehemiah 12:23; Esther 2:23). The reasons are obvious. Fragile materials, poor storage, and time cause manuscripts to be worn out, damaged, and lost (p. 26).

> But the Bible had an additional, potentially much greater, threat to its survival:
>
> repeated, willful attempts to destroy the book forever.

As we step back and objectively look at history, the Bible seems to be a battleground, a focal point between the forces of good and evil. No other book compares to the Bible regarding the commitment by some to destroy it or by others to preserve it. An overview of the battle for the Bible's survival, and of the evidence for its historical truth, provides insights that only the God of the universe could direct.

Early Persecution

Persecution of the earliest Christians is well documented by many sources both within and outside the Bible. There is virtually no disagreement or doubt by historians that the disciples of Christ both believed the resurrection of Christ had occurred and had a life-changing experience that caused them to boldly testify, suffer, and eventually die painful deaths in order to tell others. Early persecution was not over "just" the Bible (it hadn't been organized yet). It was over the truth of the resurrection of Christ.

In A.D. 64 Nero led a massive persecution of Christians in Rome when he formally blamed them for the "great fire." Paul was probably executed then. For almost 300 years Christians were executed. Christian writings were destroyed. Some non-Christian historical documents discuss the "test" to give before condemning Christians. It was simple. To be freed, people needed "only" to curse Christ and to bow down and worship the Roman emporer.[6,13] Otherwise they were executed.

The Catacombs

Beneath Rome lies a vast network of 900 miles of caves containing the graves of 7 million Christians who perished in the first three centuries. Many of those Christians were slaughtered by Nero—placed in amphitheaters to die for entertainment of the pagan world. Larger caverns were centers where people secretly worshiped. Writings on walls testify to the tremendous courage and conviction of millions who fully believed the gospel testimony. "Forgotten" for more than 1,000 years, the Catacombs were accidentally rediscovered in 1578.

What If . . . the New Testament Vanished?

Sir David Dalrymple wondered: If absolutely every New Testament copy vanished, what could we do to "find" it?

His exhaustive investigation of other (non-Bible) writings in existence from the period of A.D. 100 to A.D. 300 (overlapping the time of eyewitnesses) revealed that the entire New Testament existed in direct quotes with the exception of only eleven verses.[6]

. . . Against All Odds

Persecution Defined the New Testament

Think about it. How strong would evidence have to be to place *your* life on the line for a belief based on *historical fact?* The *historical* resurrection of Jesus Christ was *the* essential message and basis for the Christian church. Early Christians didn't have the excuse of claiming centuries of distortion. They were within (or close to) the time of eyewitnesses. New Testament documents were already an accepted body of historical fact among Christians. Their deaths confirmed it.

While early church history shows that some people recanted their faith, hoping to later repent and return to the church, *many* chose death over denying the Gospel. Obviously, such a choice would involve a very careful consideration of eyewitness testimony and the truth of the reports in circulation that clarified it (the New Testament). Would so many people choose a slow, painful death defending reports that were false or contained errors? Any reports that were in question at all were disregarded in the formation of the canon. All apostles who *knew* the truth for certain suffered the same martyr's death (except John—see p. 23).

Other Attempts to Destroy the Bible

We most commonly think about the intense persecution of the early Christians, when it would have been "easiest" to wipe out the Gospel message through execution—before it was widely accepted throughout the world. God not only succeeded in having "His Book" maintain the greatest ancient manuscript survival rate by far (see pp. 26–27), but used early testimony by death—indisputable evidence of commitment—to verify the

Edict of A.D. 303

Emperor Diocletian declared that anyone discovered with a Bible would immediately be put to death.

accuracy of the writings. Attempts to destroy the Bible don't end there. In fact, even today more than 250,000 Christians die martyrs' deaths every year for their faith. Bibles are routinely destroyed.

Muslim Countries—Christianity is banned in many areas. Martyr death is common, and Bibles are destroyed when found.

China—Still has many Christian martyrs. Until very recently there existed only one Bible per 250,000 Christians—reflecting years of Bible persecution.

Russia—Finally it is tolerant—after years of intense martyrdom. With a previous position of atheism, Bibles are a rare commodity.

Voltaire vs. God?

Voltaire, a prominent French writer and philosopher, boasted in the 1700s that within 100 years, Christianity and the Bible would disappear—implying that his works would remain much longer.

Today, few know much about Voltaire, but the Bible has constantly grown—remaining by far the bestseller for every year since its beginning.

Ironically, today Voltaire's house and printing press are used by the Geneva Bible Society to publish many Bibles.[6]

"Fingerprints" of God . . .

What does it take to convince a skeptic that God effectively "wrote" the Bible (through the influence of the Holy Spirit on human authors)? Not surprisingly, God provided His "fingerprints" throughout the Bible in many ways, quite possibly to offer evidence to the wide variety of skeptics He knew existed. This evidence ranges from basic insights provided centuries ahead of discovery by man to complex statistical proofs meaningful to highly educated mathematicians.

The Bible says it will reveal God and the truth to anyone who sincerely seeks it (Matthew 7:7; Luke 11:9). It also says that the truth will remain hidden to those with hardened hearts—that even literal resurrection from the dead will not convince them (Luke 16:27-33). The skeptic needs to ask: Am I honestly seeking the truth revealed? Or have I already made up my mind with a "hardened" heart?

Prophecy

Several times the Bible stresses the use of prophecy to determine if something is "of God" (Deuteronomy 18:22; Isaiah 41:22,23). So we would certainly expect a book inspired by God to contain prophecy—and lots of it. In fact, every *historical* prophecy in the Bible (prophecies other than end-times prophecies or heaven-related ones) that *should* have been fulfilled was fulfilled. Only one prophetic event remains now to "set the stage" for the sequence of events in Revelation. It is the rebuilding of the Temple in Jerusalem (plans are well underway to do it). Of the 667 *historical* prophecies to date, all but three can be *verified* as being fulfilled (that doesn't mean the three weren't fulfilled; we just have no record). Prophecies are often quite exact and specific. People's names are given, detailed events are outlined, and precise timing down to the year—and *even to the day*—is specified. No other holy book contains prophecy like the Bible. A few "holy books" make occasional attempts at prophecy and fail.

Scientific Insights

While the Bible isn't a book about science, one would expect it to be accurate in references concerning science even before mankind knew or discovered the facts. Not only is the Bible accurate in the smallest detail, but many scientific insights are contained within it, albeit unknown to man for centuries.

Some of these insights were given to man to help him. Noah was told the exact dimensions and design to use for the ark. No comparably sized vessel was built again until the late 1800s. And twentieth-century engineers have now calculated that the design and ratios given by God are the precise, best design for a "barge-type craft" in rough open seas.

God promised to protect His people from the deadly diseases of the Egyptians (Exodus 15:26). Principles of sanitation and quarantine, not understood until centuries later, were given to Moses. Ironically, the Black Plague of Europe caused "scientists" to look to theologians for answers. By following the laws of Moses, they helped the dreaded Black Plague finally come to an end. Other medical "secrets" and amazing insights regarding areas of physics, chemistry, geology, and astronomy are included in the Bible as well.

. . . Throughout the Bible

Creation

The account of creation alone makes the Bible unique among holy books and reveals a fingerprint of God. Genesis 1 provides an amazing, accurate account of creation that has only recently been fully confirmed by the scientific world. Some highlights of the latest evidence include:

- The order of creation events, in precise agreement with science.

- The implication of the beginning of time (Genesis 1:1; see also 2 Timothy 1:9; Titus 1:2; 1 Corinthians 2:7) now confirmed by the general theory of relativity.

Obviously, Moses had to have divine revelation just to *know* the events of creation. No other holy book contains that information. But even if the creation events were common knowledge then, the odds of his guessing the correct order was about 1 in 4 million—similar to the odds of winning a state lottery.

Concealed Evidence

God also embedded information within biblical commands and even in the letters and words themselves. This concealed evidence takes several forms. The Feasts of Israel essentially mirror the plan of redemption and confirm God's plan with the perfect verification through the death and resurrection of Jesus Christ. The *design of the tabernacle* is filled with references and symbology of the coming Savior and the precise role He would play. And even many *stories of the patriarchs* foretell the gospel message, using examples—models of people and events that

Note of Caution

Concealed evidence in the Bible does *not* mean the Bible can be used for any form of "divination"—which is strictly forbidden (Deuteronomy 18:14). It simply suggests God may have placed facts in a way that might be discovered *only after the events take place* to indicate His planning and foresight.

foreshadow the exact fulfillment by Jesus. Only upon the post-analysis of the gospel is it so obvious that God's whole plan of redemption is richly imbedded in Jewish culture.

Other probability analysis of patterns in the Bible indicates the possibility of divine planning. Both the opening verse of Genesis and the opening genealogy of Christ (in Matthew) contain an amazing number of items divisible by 7.[14] Seven seems to be used throughout the Bible as a sign of perfection, or "of God." Is it coincidence?

Some claim to have found "hidden codes" about world events embedded in the original biblical text. Such "codes" need to be evaluated with caution. While some findings may eventually prove to be valid, to date—*none* are statistically significant. "Bible Code" computer analysis of simple word-groups is deceptive. Psychics and astrologers (forbidden in the Bible) have long preyed on our human desire to believe by providing the power of suggestion with words. Someone determined to find a hidden meaning can perform extensive computer word searches until a pair of words "show up" that can be construed to make a point. On the other hand, it is conceivable that we someday may find *clearly defined, unalterable, statistically meaningful* information that indicates the hand of God.*

*See *Are There Hidden Codes in the Bible?* in the *Examine the Evidence* series.

Common Questions

What If I Don't Believe the Entire Bible?

Having a relationship with God does not depend on believing the entire Bible. Belief in and acceptance of Jesus as Savior are all that is required. Those who thoroughly investigate the Bible find abundant evidence that every claim of the Bible is true—and nearly all claims have substantial support. Even when "modern" science seems at odds with it, the Bible ultimately has proven true. But waiting to accept a relationship with Christ until *all* doubts are answered would be foolish. Your time on earth could end tomorrow. Instead, pray for insight. The truth will eventually be revealed.

How Can We Know We Will Go to Heaven?

When Jesus said not all who use His name will enter heaven (Matthew 7:21–23), He was referring to people who think using Christ's name along with rules and rituals is the key to heaven. A *relationship* with God is *not* based on rituals or rules. It's based on grace and forgiveness and the right relationship with Him.

How to Have a Personal Relationship with God

1. **B**elieve that God exists and that He came to earth in the human form of Jesus Christ (John 3:16; Romans 10:9).

2. **A**ccept God's free forgiveness of sins through the death and resurrection of Jesus Christ (Ephesians 2:8-10; 1:7,8).

3. **S**witch to God's plan for your life (1 Peter 1:21-23; Ephesians 2:1-5).

4. **E**xpress desire for Christ to be director of your life (Matthew 7:21-27; 1 John 4:15).

Prayer for Eternal Life with God

Dear God, I believe You sent Your Son, Jesus, to die for my sins so I can be forgiven. I'm sorry for my sins, and I want to live the rest of my life the way You want me to. Please put Your Spirit in my life to direct me. Amen.

Then What?

People who sincerely take the above steps become members of God's family of believers. A new world of freedom and strength is available through prayer and obedience to God's will. New members of God's family can build their relationship with God by following these steps:

- Find a Bible-based church that you like, and attend regularly.

- Set aside some time each day to pray and read the Bible.

- Locate other Christians to spend time with on a regular basis.

God's Promises to Believers

For Today

"But seek first his kingdom and his righteousness, and all these things [things to satisfy all your needs] will be given to you as well" (Matthew 6:33).

For Eternity

"Whoever believes in the Son has eternal life, but whoever rejects the Son will not see life, for God's wrath remains on him" (John 3:36).

Once we develop an eternal perspective, even the greatest problems on earth fade in significance.

Notes

1. Muncaster, Ralph O., *The Bible—Creation versus Evolution—Investigation of the Evidence*, Mission Viejo, CA: Strong Basis to Believe, Inc., 1997.

2. Muncaster, Ralph O., *The Bible—Prophecy Miracles—Investigation of the Evidence*, Mission Viejo, CA: Strong Basis to Believe, Inc., 1996.

3. Muncaster, Ralph O., *The Bible—Scientific Insights—Investigation of the Evidence*, Mission Viejo, CA: Strong Basis to Believe, Inc., 1996.

4. McDowell, Josh, *Evidence that Demands a Verdict—Vol. I*, Nashville, TN: Thomas Nelson, Inc., 1979.

5. McDowell, Josh, *Evidence that Demands a Verdict—Vol. II*, Nashville, TN: Thomas Nelson, Inc., 1979.

6. McDowell, Josh and Wilson, Bill, *A Ready Defense*, San Bernardino, CA: Here's Life Publishers, Inc., 1990.

7. Bruce, F. F., *The Canon of Scripture*, Downers Grove, IL: InterVarsity Press, 1988.

8. Comfort, Philip Wesley, ed., *The Origin of the Bible*, Wheaton, IL: Tyndale House Publishers, 1992.

9. Scott, Julius J., PhD., *Life and Teachings of Jesus*, audiotape, Wheaton, IL: Wheaton College Graduate School Extension Studies, 1988.

10. Youngblood, Ronald F, *New Illustrated Bible Dictionary*, Nashville, TN: Abingdon, 1996.

11. Jefferies, Grant R., *The Signature of God*, Toronto, Ontario, Canada: Frontier Research Publications, 1996.

12. Shanks, Hershel, ed., *Understanding the Dead Sea Scrolls*, New York, NY: Vintage Books, 1993.

13. Vos, Howard F., *Introduction to Church History*, Nashville, TN: Abingdon, 1994.

14. Missler, Chuck, *The Creator Beyond Time and Space*, Costa Mesa, CA: The Word for Today, 1996.

Bibliography

Bruce, F. F., *The History of the Bible in English*, New York, NY: Oxford Press, 1978.

Eastman, Mark, MD, and Missler, Chuck, *The Creator Beyond Time and Space*, Costa Mesa, CA: The Word for Today, 1996.

Encyclopedia Britannica, Chicago, IL: 1993.

Life Application Bible, Wheaton, IL: Tyndale House Publishers, and Grand Rapids, MI: Zondervan Publishing House, 1991.

Packer, J. I., Tenney, Merrill C., and White, William Jr., *Illustrated Encyclopedia of Bible Facts*, Nashville, TN: Thomas Nelson, Inc., 1980.

Phillips, John, *Exploring the World of the Jew*, Neptune, NJ: Loizeaux Brothers, 1993.

Rambsel, Yacov, *Yeshua*, Toronto, Ontario, Canada: Frontier Research Publications, 1996.

Rosen, Moishe, *Y'shua*, Chicago, IL: Moody Bible Institute, 1982.

Shepherd, Coulson, *Jewish Holy Days*, Neptune, NJ: Loizeaux Brothers, 1961.

Strauss, Lehman, *God's Prophetic Calendar*, Neptune, NJ: Loizeaux Brothers, 1987.

Smith, F. LaGard, *The Daily Bible in Chronological Order*, Eugene, OR: Harvest House, 1984.

Walvoord, John F, *The Prophecy Knowledge Handbook*, Wheaton, IL: Victor Books, 1990.